# VICTIMOLOGY
# UNVEILED

# VICTIMOLOGY UNVEILED

PATRICK MORGAN

# CONTENTS

# CHAPTER 1

# Introduction to Victimology

*Definition and Scope of Victimology*

Victimology is a specialized field within criminology that focuses on understanding the role of victims in the context of crime, particularly violent crimes such as murder. This subchapter will define victimology and explore its scope, emphasizing how it relates to various aspects of victim selection in murder cases. Victimology examines not only the characteristics of victims but also the social, psychological, and situational factors that contribute to their vulnerability. This understanding is crucial for true crime enthusiasts who seek to analyze the motives and methods of murderers through the lens of their chosen victims.

At its core, victimology seeks to answer questions about why certain individuals are targeted by criminals. It investigates the traits and circumstances that make some people more susceptible to becoming victims than others. This includes an exploration of demographic factors such as age, gender, and socioeconomic status, as well as psychological profiles that may influence a potential victim's behavior and lifestyle. By delving into these characteristics, true crime enthusiasts can gain insights into the minds of both the victim and the perpetrator, shedding light on the complex dynamics at play in murder cases.

The geographic considerations of victim selection are another critical aspect of victimology. The environment in which a potential victim resides can significantly influence their likelihood of being targeted. Urban areas may present different risks compared to rural settings, and factors such as proximity to crime hotspots, social networks, and local crime rates all play a role in determining vulnerability. True crime enthusiasts can analyze historical case studies to identify patterns in geographic victim selection, providing a richer understanding of how location impacts the dynamics of murder.

Social dynamics further complicate the landscape of victim selection. An individual's relationships, social status, and community ties can either shield them from or expose them to criminal threats. Vulnerability can arise from factors such as isolation, lack of support systems, or engagement in risky behaviors. By examining these social elements, true crime enthusiasts can better appreciate the interplay between the victim's environment and their likelihood of being chosen. This perspective enhances the understanding of how murderers exploit social dynamics to identify and select their victims.

Finally, the impact of technology on victim accessibility cannot be overlooked. With the rise of digital platforms and social media, potential victims may inadvertently expose themselves to dangers by sharing personal information or engaging in behaviors that attract unwanted attention. Victimology also explores the role of forensic evidence in understanding victim selection strategies employed by murderers. By analyzing how technology and forensic advancements influence the selection and profiling of victims, true crime enthusiasts can gain a comprehensive view of the evolving landscape of crime and victimization, enriching their appreciation for the complex narratives surrounding murder cases.

*Historical Context of Victim Selection*

The historical context of victim selection in murder cases reveals a complex interplay of societal norms, individual psychology, and the broader environment. Throughout history, the choice of victims has been influenced by various factors, including cultural attitudes towards violence, the perceived value of certain demographics, and the social structures that dictate power dynamics. In ancient societies, for instance, sacrificial victims were often chosen based on their societal roles or religious significance, reflecting community beliefs and practices. As societies evolved, the motivations behind victim selection transitioned from ritualistic to more personal or opportunistic motivations, influenced by changing social structures and the rise of individualism.

Psychological profiles of potential victims have also evolved over time, with certain characteristics making individuals more susceptible to becoming targets. In the early 20th century, for instance, the emergence of psychological theories began to shed light on the traits that might indicate vulnerability, such as isolation or socio-economic status. These profiles have been further refined in contemporary times, with an increasing understanding of how factors like mental health, lifestyle choices, and personal relationships can contribute to an individual's likelihood of being targeted. Understanding these psychological dimensions is essential for true crime enthusiasts, as they highlight the intricate relationship between victim characteristics and the motivations of offenders.

Geographic considerations play a crucial role in victim selection, with historical patterns revealing how location can significantly impact vulnerability. Urban areas, with their anonymity and dense populations, have often been seen as hunting grounds for offenders. Conversely, rural regions might present different challenges and opportunities for both victims and perpetrators. Historical case studies illustrate how the geography of crime has shifted over time, influenced by urbanization, migration patterns, and changes in law enforcement practices. True crime enthusiasts can delve into these geographic dynamics to better understand how location can dictate victim selection and the types of crimes that emerge within different environments.

Social dynamics and victim vulnerability have been paramount in shaping who becomes a target. Throughout history, marginalized groups often bear the brunt of violent crimes, as societal attitudes can render them more vulnerable and less likely to receive justice. This pattern is evident in numerous historical case studies, where victims from lower socio-economic backgrounds, racial minorities, or those perceived as outsiders have been disproportionately affected. The social context surrounding these individuals plays a significant role in their victimization, often influenced by factors such as community support, media representation, and societal values. By examining these dynamics, true crime enthusiasts can gain insight into the broader implications of social structures on victim selection.

The role of opportunity in victim selection cannot be overstated, as historical trends show that many murders are committed impulsively, driven by chance encounters rather than premeditated planning. Factors such as accessibility, routine behaviors, and situational vulnerabilities often dictate who becomes a victim. The advent of technology has further transformed this landscape, making individuals more accessible through social media and digital communication. This evolution poses new challenges in understanding victim selection, as offenders may exploit online platforms to identify and target potential victims. By analyzing the historical and contemporary shifts in opportunity and accessibility, true crime enthusiasts can better comprehend the intricate strategies involved in victim selection and the ongoing impact of technological advancements on crime.

*Importance of Studying Victim Choices*

Understanding the choices made by victims in the context of crime is an essential aspect of victimology that provides insights into the broader dynamics of criminal behavior. Victim choices are influenced by a complex interplay of psychological, social, and environmental factors. Analyzing these choices helps in comprehending why certain individuals become targets, which can be crucial for prevention efforts. For true crime enthusiasts, delving into the intricacies of victim selection not only enhances their understanding of criminal motives but also fosters a deeper appreciation for the factors that contribute to vulnerability in society.

Psychological profiles of potential victims are a key area of study within victimology. Certain personality traits, behaviors, and circumstances can make individuals more susceptible to becoming victims. By examining historical case studies, enthusiasts can identify patterns and commonalities among victims that may reveal underlying psychological vulnerabilities. This understanding is vital for both law enforcement and communities in developing targeted outreach programs aimed at educating potential victims about risks and improving their resilience against crime.

Geographic considerations also play a significant role in victim choice. The environment in which individuals live can greatly influence their likelihood of being targeted. Urban areas, for instance, may present different risks compared to rural communities due to population density, socio-economic factors, and crime rates. True crime enthusiasts can benefit from exploring how geographic dynamics shape victimization patterns, allowing for a more nuanced understanding of the spatial elements that contribute to crime.

Social dynamics and victim vulnerability are intricately linked, as societal structures often dictate who is more likely to be victimized. Factors such as age, gender, and socio-economic status can affect an individual's risk of becoming a target. By analyzing historical trends and contemporary examples, enthusiasts can grasp how social hierarchies and cultural norms influence victim selection. This knowledge can inform discussions about societal responsibility and the importance of creating supportive environments that minimize vulnerabilities.

Lastly, the role of opportunity in victim selection cannot be overstated. Criminals often exploit situations where victims are most accessible, making it essential to consider how technology and societal changes impact victim accessibility. The rise of digital interactions, for example, has introduced new avenues for victimization, necessitating an exploration of how technological advancements alter traditional patterns of crime. True crime enthusiasts can gain valuable insights by examining these evolving dynamics, which underscore the importance of studying victim choices to develop proactive measures aimed at enhancing safety and reducing victimization in society.

# CHAPTER 2

# How to Pick a Murder Victim

*Psychological Factors in Victim Selection*

Psychological factors play a crucial role in the selection of victims by offenders, shaping the dynamics of criminal behavior and influencing the choices made in the heat of the moment. Understanding these factors requires delving into the cognitive and emotional processes that drive an offender's decision-making. Many murderers exhibit certain psychological traits that guide them toward specific types of victims. These traits can include a desire for power, control, or revenge, often leading to a preference for individuals who are perceived as vulnerable or defenseless. This psychological predilection often manifests in the offender's selection criteria, highlighting the importance of understanding the mental framework that underpins these choices.

Victim selection is also heavily influenced by psychological profiles that offenders create, either consciously or subconsciously. Offenders may seek out victims who share characteristics with past figures in their lives, such as abusive family members or unrequited loves. This identification can lead to a tragic cycle of violence, where the victim unwittingly embodies the traits of someone who has caused the offender emotional pain. In this context, the victim becomes a stand-in for unresolved psychological conflicts, making the act of murder a misguided attempt at reclaiming control or closure. Such psychological motivations underscore the complexity of offender behavior, illustrating that the choice of victim is often as much about the offender's internal struggles as it is about external circumstances.

Geographic considerations further compound the psychological factors at play in victim selection.

Offenders often target victims within familiar environments, where they perceive greater control and less risk of apprehension. This familiarity can provide a false sense of security, reinforcing the psychological motivations behind their choices. Furthermore, certain areas may be associated with specific demographic characteristics, making it easier for offenders to identify potential victims who fit their psychological profiles. This geographic predilection emphasizes the importance of location in the victim selection process, as it not only impacts the offender's logistics but also their emotional comfort in committing the crime.

Social dynamics and victim vulnerability are also critical in understanding how psychological factors influence victim selection. Offenders may specifically seek out individuals who exhibit signs of social isolation, such as those with limited support networks or those facing personal crises. The psychological profile of the offender often dictates the perceived vulnerability of the potential victim. For instance, individuals who are perceived as weak or submissive may be targeted because they are considered easier to control. This interplay between the offender's psychological state and the victim's social standing creates a dangerous environment where certain individuals are disproportionately at risk of becoming victims.

Historical case studies provide valuable insights into the patterns of victim selection influenced by psychological factors. Analyzing notorious cases reveals recurring themes, such as the targeting of specific demographics based on the offender's past experiences or societal beliefs. These studies often highlight the chilling reality that many murderers are not random in their choices; rather, they operate within a framework of psychological logic that informs their actions. By examining these historical instances, true crime enthusiasts can gain a deeper understanding of the multifaceted nature of victim selection, recognizing that behind each crime lies a complex web of psychological, social, and environmental influences that shape the choices made by both offenders and their victims.

*Behavioral Patterns of Offenders*

Behavioral patterns of offenders are crucial in understanding the dynamics of victim selection in murder cases. Offenders often exhibit predictable behaviors that can be analyzed to reveal their preferences and methods. These patterns can include the types of victims they choose, the circumstances under which they commit their crimes, and the psychological motivations driving their actions. By examining these behaviors, true crime enthusiasts can gain insights into why certain individuals become targets while others do not, and how offenders capitalize on vulnerabilities in their victims.

One prominent aspect of the offender's behavior is their psychological profile, which can reveal preferred victim characteristics. Many offenders gravitate toward individuals who display certain traits, such as vulnerability, isolation, or a lack of social support. For example, those with low self-esteem or who are perceived as easy targets often become victims because offenders believe they can exert control over them. Understanding these psychological profiles not only sheds light on victim selection but also emphasizes the importance of awareness and self-protection for potential targets.

Geographic considerations also play a significant role in the behavioral patterns of offenders.

Many murderers operate within familiar environments, such as neighborhoods or social circles, where they can assess potential victims' routines and vulnerabilities. This geographic familiarity allows offenders to plan their actions more effectively and increases their chances of success. True crime enthusiasts should consider how an offender's choice of location influences their selection of victims and the methods they employ to commit their crimes.

Social dynamics further complicate the picture of victim vulnerability. Offenders often exploit existing social structures to identify and target victims. For instance, individuals who are marginalized due to factors like socioeconomic status, race, or gender may be more susceptible to violence. Additionally, offenders may take advantage of social situations, such as parties or gatherings, where potential victims can be more easily isolated. Understanding these social dynamics is essential for recognizing the broader societal factors that contribute to victimization.

Historical case studies provide a wealth of information on the behavioral patterns of offenders and their victim choices. Analyzing infamous cases allows for a deeper understanding of how these patterns manifest in real-life scenarios. For example, examining the choices of serial killers can reveal consistent themes in victim selection, such as age, appearance, or lifestyle. By studying these historical precedents, true crime enthusiasts can develop a nuanced understanding of how opportunity, technology, and demographic factors interplay in the complex web of victimization.

*Risk Assessment in Victim Targeting*

Risk assessment in victim targeting is a critical component in understanding the dynamics of homicide. This process involves evaluating various factors that contribute to the selection of victims by offenders. True crime enthusiasts often delve into the psychological profiles of potential victims, examining traits that may make individuals more susceptible to violence. Offenders may target those perceived as vulnerable due to factors such as age, socioeconomic status, or mental health. Recognizing these patterns can provide insight into the risk factors that influence an assailant's choice.

Geographic considerations also play a significant role in victim selection. Offenders often operate within familiar environments where they can assess potential targets with less scrutiny. The proximity to the victim's home or a location frequented by the offender can significantly increase the likelihood of selection. Crime statistics frequently reveal patterns related to specific neighborhoods, where certain demographics may experience higher rates of victimization. Understanding these geographic dynamics is essential for identifying at-risk populations and implementing preventative measures.

Social dynamics further complicate the landscape of victim targeting. The relationships individuals maintain can either shield them from danger or expose them to risk. For example, those involved in high-risk lifestyles, such as drug use or criminal activity, may attract violence. Additionally, societal perceptions of strength or vulnerability can shift based on social circles, influencing how offenders select their victims. This interplay between an individual's social environment and their perceived vulnerability is crucial in assessing risk.

Historical case studies of victim choice reveal consistent trends that persist across time. By examining infamous cases, true crime enthusiasts can identify common characteristics among victims and the circumstances surrounding their deaths. These studies often highlight the role of opportunity, where the timing and location of an encounter drastically impact the likelihood of victimization. Analyzing these factors within historical contexts provides a framework for understanding contemporary victim targeting.

The impact of technology cannot be understated in the realm of victim accessibility. Advances in communication and social media have altered how offenders identify and approach potential victims. Online platforms can provide insights into an individual's life, making it easier for an offender to assess vulnerability. Furthermore, forensic evidence has evolved, bringing new strategies to light, allowing investigators to understand not only how victims were chosen but also the methods employed by offenders. This technological interplay emphasizes the need for ongoing risk assessment strategies that adapt to changing societal land-scapes.

# CHAPTER 3

# Psychological Profiles of Potential Victims

*Characteristics of High-Risk Individuals*

High-risk individuals often exhibit distinct characteristics that make them more susceptible to becoming victims of violent crimes, particularly murder. Understanding these traits is crucial for true crime enthusiasts who seek to comprehend the dynamics of victim selection. Common characteristics include social isolation, vulnerability due to lifestyle choices, and specific demographic factors. Individuals who live alone or lack strong social networks often find themselves at greater risk, as their isolation can make them easier targets for potential offenders. Additionally, those engaged in high-risk behaviors, such as substance abuse or involvement in criminal activities, may inadvertently attract violent encounters.

Psychological profiles of high-risk individuals reveal patterns that can enhance vulnerability. Many victims may display low self-esteem or a history of trauma, which can impede their ability to recognize or respond to dangerous situations. This psychological disposition can lead them to make poor choices regarding their safety, such as ignoring warning signs or remaining in unsafe environments. Furthermore, individuals with mental health issues may struggle to assert themselves in confrontational situations, making them less likely to escape dangerous interactions. Recognizing these psychological factors is vital in understanding how certain individuals become targets.

Geographic considerations also play a significant role in identifying high-risk individuals. Urban areas, particularly those with high crime rates, present unique challenges and dangers. Victims may find themselves in neighborhoods where violence is more prevalent and where the likelihood of encountering individuals with harmful intentions increases. Moreover, the time of day can influence risk, as certain locations may be safer during daylight hours but become perilous after dark. True crime enthusiasts can learn from historical case studies that illustrate how geographical factors contribute to victim selection and the patterns that emerge in specific locales.

Social dynamics further complicate the landscape of victim vulnerability. Individuals from marginalized communities or those lacking support systems can be particularly at risk. Factors such as socioeconomic status, race, and gender often intersect, shaping the experiences of potential victims. In many instances, societal attitudes and biases can lead to neglect or a lack of protective measures for these high-risk groups. Understanding the social context surrounding victimization is essential for true crime enthusiasts to grasp the broader implications of crime and its impact on various demographics.

Finally, the advancement of technology has transformed the ways in which potential victims can be targeted. Online platforms, social media, and dating apps have created new avenues for offenders to identify and exploit vulnerabilities. High-risk individuals may unknowingly share personal information that makes them accessible to predators. Additionally, the anonymity of the internet can embolden offenders, making it easier for them to engage in predatory behavior. For true crime enthusiasts, exploring the intersection of technology and victim selection offers valuable insights into the evolving nature of crime and the continuing challenges faced by vulnerable individuals.

### *The Role of Vulnerability in Selection*

The concept of vulnerability plays a crucial role in the selection of murder victims, as it often dictates the ease with which a perpetrator can carry out their intentions. Vulnerability can manifest in various forms, including physical, psychological, and social aspects. Perpetrators tend to target individuals who exhibit signs of weakness or lack of support systems, making them more susceptible to predation. This selection process is not merely arbitrary; it is calculated, rooted in the offender's understanding of human behavior and the environment surrounding potential victims.

Psychological profiles of potential victims reveal that those suffering from mental health issues or exhibiting signs of social isolation are often at a heightened risk. Offenders may perceive these victims as less likely to resist or report the crime. The psychological state of a victim can significantly influence their behavior and decision-making, rendering them more vulnerable to manipulation or coercion. Understanding the psychological dimensions of victim selection is essential for comprehending why certain individuals become targets while others do not.

Geographic considerations also play a significant role in determining vulnerability. Areas with high crime rates, limited community resources, or lack of surveillance can create environments where potential victims are more exposed. Offenders often scout locations where they can find individuals who are less likely to attract attention or where escape routes are readily available. These geographic factors can be compounded by social dynamics, where victims from marginalized communities may face increased risks due to systemic inequalities and lack of protective resources.

Social dynamics further complicate the issue of vulnerability in victim selection. Individuals who lack strong social networks or support systems are often seen as easier targets. Factors such as socioeconomic status, gender, and age influence a victim's vulnerability, with certain demographics being more susceptible to violent crime. The interplay of these social elements can create a landscape where specific individuals are disproportionately at risk, highlighting the need for a deeper understanding of how societal structures affect victimization.

Historical case studies provide valuable insights into the patterns of victim selection based on vulnerability. Analyzing previous murder cases reveals consistent trends in how offenders identify and exploit their victims' weaknesses. These studies underscore the importance of recognizing vulnerability not only as a characteristic of potential victims but also as a critical factor that drives the decision-making process of offenders. By examining these cases, true crime enthusiasts can gain a more nuanced understanding of the complexities surrounding victim selection and the broader implications for society.

*Psychological Manipulation and Victimization*

Psychological manipulation plays a critical role in the dynamics of victimization, particularly in the context of murder. Manipulators often exploit vulnerabilities in potential victims, employing tactics that involve deception, emotional coercion, and psychological pressure. By understanding the intricacies of psychological manipulation, true crime enthusiasts can gain insights into the methods employed by offenders to select and target victims. This subchapter delves into these manipulative strategies, emphasizing their implications in the broader scope of victimology.

The psychological profiles of potential victims reveal significant patterns that manipulators exploit. Victims often exhibit traits such as low self-esteem, social isolation, or a history of trauma, making them more susceptible to manipulation.

Offenders can identify these characteristics through various means, including observation and social interaction. By assessing a victim's psychological state, they can tailor their approach, using charm or empathy to establish trust before exploiting their vulnerabilities. This understanding underscores the importance of recognizing psychological indicators that may signal a potential victim's susceptibility to manipulation.

Geographic considerations also play a vital role in the selection of victims. Certain environments may foster conditions that heighten an individual's vulnerability to manipulation and subsequent victimization. For instance, areas with poor social cohesion, high crime rates, or a lack of community resources can create fertile ground for offenders. Manipulators may take advantage of these geographic factors, knowing that potential victims are less likely to receive assistance or support when needed. This geographic context is essential for understanding how location influences both the accessibility of victims and the psychological tactics employed by offenders.

Social dynamics further complicate the landscape of victim vulnerability. Interpersonal relationships, peer influences, and community structures can significantly impact an individual's susceptibility to psychological manipulation. Offenders often exploit social norms or group dynamics to isolate their targets, making them more dependent on the manipulator. For example, an individual who is ostracized by peers may find themselves drawn to a manipulative figure who offers companionship or acceptance, ultimately leading to victimization. This interplay between social dynamics and psychological manipulation highlights the need for a nuanced understanding of victim selection processes.

Historical case studies provide valuable insights into the patterns of victim choice influenced by psychological manipulation. By examining notorious cases, true crime enthusiasts can identify common tactics employed by offenders across different contexts and eras. These studies reveal how manipulators have adapted their strategies to exploit societal changes, technological advancements, and evolving psychological understandings. The lessons drawn from these historical examples not only enhance our comprehension of victimology but also serve as cautionary tales, emphasizing the importance of awareness and resilience in the face of potential psychological manipulation.

# CHAPTER 4

# Geographic Considerations in Victim Selection

*Crime Hotspots and Their Influence*

Crime hotspots are geographic areas where the incidence of crime is significantly higher than in surrounding regions. These locations often emerge due to a combination of social, economic, and environmental factors that create conditions conducive to criminal activity. Understanding crime hotspots is crucial for examining victimology, particularly in the context of murder choices. These areas frequently attract specific types of offenders and, consequently, a particular demographic of victims. The intersection of opportunity, vulnerability, and accessibility in these zones can provide valuable insights into the patterns of victim selection.

The psychological profiles of potential victims can be heavily influenced by their presence in these crime hotspots. Individuals living in or frequenting these areas may display certain behavioral traits, such as risk-taking or a lack of awareness regarding their surroundings, which can increase their vulnerability. Offenders often seek out victims who exhibit signs of weakness or unawareness, making crime hotspots a fertile ground for such predatory behavior. The social dynamics at play in these locations, including factors like socioeconomic status and community cohesion, can further impact who becomes a target for violence.

Geographic considerations in victim selection highlight how the physical environment contributes to the likelihood of an individual becoming a victim. Certain neighborhoods may have poorly lit streets, abandoned buildings, or a lack of security measures, all of which can make individuals more accessible to offenders. Additionally, the transient nature of populations in urban hotspots can mean that potential victims are less likely to have strong social networks or support systems, leaving them isolated and more susceptible to crime. This geographical analysis is essential for understanding the situational factors that influence who is targeted.

Social dynamics play a significant role in victim vulnerability within crime hotspots. Factors such as age, gender, and social status can impact how individuals navigate these environments. Young adults and marginalized groups often face higher risks due to societal perceptions and stereotypes that can dehumanize them in the eyes of potential offenders. Moreover, the presence of gangs or organized crime in these areas can create a culture of fear, further isolating individuals and reducing their chances of seeking help or reporting crimes, thereby perpetuating a cycle of victimization.

The role of opportunity in victim selection cannot be overstated, particularly in crime hotspots. Offenders often capitalize on circumstances that make it easier to commit crimes without facing immediate consequences. This includes the presence of technology, such as mobile devices and social media, which can inadvertently signal a person's location and availability to potential attackers. Historical case studies reveal that certain murder cases have frequently occurred in specific hotspots, underscoring the importance of understanding these dynamics in the broader context of victimology. By examining these patterns, true crime enthusiasts can gain deeper insights into how various factors converge to influence victim selection and the tragic outcomes that can follow.

*Urban vs. Rural Targeting*

Urban environments often present a unique landscape for potential murderers, influenced by dense populations, anonymity, and a variety of social dynamics. In cities, the high concentration of individuals can lead to increased opportunities for crime, as perpetrators may feel less accountable in a bustling crowd. Urban targeting often aligns with specific victim profiles that reflect the complexities of city life. Victims may be chosen based on their perceived vulnerability, which can include factors such as socioeconomic status, lifestyle choices, or even their daily routines. The anonymity of urban spaces can embolden offenders, as they can blend into the crowd after committing their crimes, making detection more challenging.

In contrast, rural areas typically exhibit different dynamics that influence victim selection. With lower population densities, perpetrators may be more likely to target individuals who are isolated or engaged in predictable patterns of life. Social ties in rural communities can complicate the landscape of victim selection, as offenders might be familiar with their victims, leading to crimes of passion or opportunistic attacks. The limited law enforcement presence in many rural settings can also create a perception of safety for the offender, potentially increasing their confidence in selecting targets who may be less likely to receive immediate assistance.

Psychological profiles play a critical role in understanding why certain individuals are targeted in urban versus rural settings. In urban contexts, offenders may seek victims who exhibit signs of vulnerability—such as individuals under the influence of drugs or those who are transient. The anonymity of city life allows these perpetrators to exploit their victims without fear of immediate repercussions. Conversely, in rural areas, attackers may select victims based on personal relationships or community status, where familiarity can breed contempt, leading to more intimate forms of violence. Understanding these psychological dimensions can help in profiling potential victims and recognizing patterns in victimization.

Geographic considerations also significantly impact victim selection strategies. Urban areas often offer a multitude of hiding places, making it easier for offenders to evade law enforcement after a crime. The availability of public transportation and the presence of nightlife can contribute to a greater pool of potential victims, as individuals may let their guard down in social settings. In rural areas, geographic isolation means that victims may be more exposed and vulnerable, particularly in the absence of immediate neighbors or witnesses. The distinct geography of urban versus rural settings not only affects the logistics of committing a crime but also shapes the profile of potential victims.

Historical case studies provide valuable insights into the patterns of victim selection across urban and rural environments. Analyzing infamous murders can reveal how location impacts the choice of victims and the offender's modus operandi. Cases like the Zodiac Killer in urban San Francisco highlight the interplay of anonymity and opportunity, while the tragic story of rural serial killers often underscores the intimate knowledge of the community that these offenders possess. By examining these historical precedents, true crime enthusiasts can gain a deeper understanding of the factors that influence victim targeting, shedding light on the broader implications of social dynamics, geography, and individual psychology in the realm of victimology.

*Environmental Factors in Victim Location*

Environmental factors play a crucial role in the dynamics of victim location, influencing how and why specific individuals become targets for murder. Geographic considerations, such as the physical landscape, urban versus rural settings, and population density, can significantly affect a perpetrator's decision-making process. In dense urban environments, for example, the anonymity provided by crowds can embolden offenders, while remote areas may present fewer opportunities but might attract those seeking isolation from potential witnesses. Understanding the interplay between these environmental variables helps in dissecting the choices made by murderers when selecting their victims.

In addition to geographic settings, social dynamics within a community can dictate victim vulnerability. Neighborhood characteristics, such as socioeconomic status, crime rates, and social cohesion, can create environments where certain individuals are perceived as easier targets. For instance, areas with high levels of poverty may see a rise in violent crime, as offenders may view those struggling economically as more accessible or less likely to report crimes. Conversely, communities with strong social ties may deter criminal activity, as the increased vigilance of neighbors can serve as a protective factor for potential victims.

The role of opportunity is also a significant environmental factor in victim selection. Opportunities for crime often arise from situational contexts, such as the presence of potential victims in secluded locations or during vulnerable times, like late at night. Offenders might scout locations for signs of opportunity, such as unlocked doors, unattended vehicles, or individuals engaged in risky behaviors. The ability to assess and exploit these situational cues demonstrates how environmental factors can dictate not only the choice of victims but also the likelihood of successful criminal acts.

Technological advancements have transformed the landscape of victim accessibility, impacting how murderers locate and select their targets. The proliferation of social media, location-based services, and online interactions has created new avenues for offenders to identify potential victims. For example, individuals who frequently share their whereabouts or personal details online may inadvertently expose themselves to danger. As technology continues to evolve, so too do the strategies employed by criminals, making it vital for both law enforcement and the general public to remain vigilant regarding the implications of their digital footprints.

Historical case studies reveal how environmental factors have shaped the choices of murderers across different contexts and time periods. Analyzing notorious cases, such as those involving serial killers or targeted hate crimes, highlights patterns in victim selection that correlate with environmental influences. These studies not only provide insight into the motivations behind such heinous acts but also serve as cautionary tales that underscore the importance of understanding the multifaceted relationship between environment and victimization. By exploring these historical perspectives, true crime enthusiasts can gain a deeper comprehension of the complexities involved in the process of victim selection.

# CHAPTER 5

# Social Dynamics and Victim Vulnerability

*The Impact of Social Networks*

The advent of social networks has revolutionized how individuals interact and connect with one another, creating both opportunities and challenges in the realm of victimology. True crime enthusiasts often analyze how social media platforms facilitate communication and information sharing, enabling potential offenders to gather insights into their targets. A victim's online presence can reveal personal details, such as their interests, routines, and social circles, making them more accessible to those with malicious intent. This newfound visibility can amplify vulnerability, as individuals inadvertently disclose information that could be exploited for predatory behavior.

In understanding the psychological profiles of potential victims, social networks play a crucial role. Users often curate their online personas, projecting images of confidence or seeking validation through likes and shares. However, this desire for connection can also expose insecurities, making certain individuals appear more susceptible to manipulation. Offenders may use this knowledge to identify those who exhibit traits such as loneliness or a need for affirmation, thereby honing in on individuals who may be less likely to resist unwanted advances or criminal acts.

Geographic considerations also become intertwined with the influence of social networks. Platforms often allow for location tagging and public sharing of events, which can inadvertently broadcast an individual's whereabouts to a wider audience. This geographic transparency can be particularly dangerous for those who frequent public spaces or participate in social gatherings. Offenders can leverage this information to track potential victims, increasing the likelihood of pre-meditated attacks based on real-time data about a person's location and activities.

The social dynamics inherent in online inter-actions can further exacerbate victim vulnerability. Cyberbullying, harassment, and stalking have be-come prevalent issues within social networks, of-ten leading to real-world consequences. The anonymity provided by the internet can embolden offenders, as they may perceive themselves as de-tached from their actions. Victims of online harass-ment may face psychological distress, which can manifest in real-life situations, making them less alert to potential threats in their environment. This dynamic underscores how the digital realm can create a feedback loop that heightens the risk of victimization.

Historical case studies illustrate the profound impact of social networks on victim choice and se-lection. Analyzing cases where offenders utilized online platforms to identify and stalk their victims reveals patterns that can inform contemporary understandings of crime. For instance, instances where killers have engaged with their victims through social media prior to an attack highlight the intersection of technology and traditional victim selection strategies. By examining these historical precedents, true crime enthusiasts can gain deeper insights into how social networks have transformed the landscape of victimology, shaping both the opportunities for crime and the profiles of those who fall prey to it.

*Economic Factors and Victimization*

Economic factors play a pivotal role in the dynamics of victimization, influencing both the selection of victims and the context in which crimes occur. Socioeconomic status can determine a potential victim's vulnerability, as individuals from lower-income backgrounds may lack the resources for personal security and support systems. In economically disadvantaged neighborhoods, crime rates often soar, resulting in a higher likelihood of victimization. This environment creates an opportunity for offenders who may perceive these individuals as easier targets, highlighting the correlation between economic conditions and the actualization of crime.

The relationship between economic disparity and victimization extends beyond mere opportunity; it also encompasses psychological factors. Individuals experiencing economic hardship may exhibit behaviors associated with stress and desperation, which can attract potential offenders. For example, those facing financial crises may resort to high-risk activities, such as drug use or engaging in criminal enterprises, increasing their chances of becoming victims. Furthermore, the mental toll of economic instability can lead to a diminished sense of awareness and caution, further exposing these individuals to predatory behaviors.

Geographic considerations are inherently tied to economic factors, as income levels often vary significantly across different regions. Urban areas with concentrated poverty tend to experience higher crime rates, leading to a greater pool of potential victims. Conversely, affluent neighborhoods, while not immune to crime, may see a different type of victimization, often associated with property crimes rather than personal assaults. Understanding the geographical distribution of wealth and poverty is essential for analyzing how economic factors shape victim selection and the types of crimes committed in various locales.

Social dynamics also intertwine with economic factors, as community cohesion can significantly impact victim vulnerability. In economically stable communities, social networks tend to be stronger, providing a layer of protection for residents. Conversely, in areas marked by economic decline, social disintegration often leads to isolation, making individuals more susceptible to victimization. Offenders may exploit these weakened social structures, perceiving isolated individuals as prime targets. This underscores the importance of considering not just economic indicators but also the social fabric of a community when assessing victimization risks.

Lastly, historical case studies reveal how economic factors have influenced patterns of victim selection over time. Analyzing past crimes through the lens of economic conditions provides insights into the motivations behind victim choices. For instance, during periods of economic downturn, crime rates often spike, with offenders targeting those perceived as vulnerable due to their socioeconomic status. These historical perspectives not only illustrate the enduring relationship between economic conditions and victimization but also serve as a cautionary tale about the need for societal awareness and intervention in addressing the root causes of vulnerability.

*Cultural Influences on Victim Selection*

Cultural influences play a significant role in the selection of victims for murder, shaping the perceived value of individuals based on societal norms, values, and historical context. In various cultures, certain demographics are often viewed as more vulnerable or less valued, directly impacting who becomes a target for violent crime. These cultural perceptions can be influenced by factors such as ethnicity, socioeconomic status, and gender roles, with certain groups being more susceptible to victimization based on the prevailing attitudes within a community. Understanding these cultural nuances is essential for comprehending the motivations behind specific victim choices.

Psychological profiles of potential victims are often molded by cultural narratives that define what is considered desirable or undesirable behavior. In societies that stigmatize certain lifestyles, individuals embodying those traits may become prime targets for offenders. For instance, marginalized groups, such as those within the LGBTQ+ community or those facing economic hardships, may be viewed through a lens of prejudice that informs a killer's decision to select them as victims. This process reveals how cultural biases can not only influence perceptions of worth but also create environments where certain lives are deemed expendable, thus impacting victim selection.

Geographic considerations further intersect with cultural influences, as the dynamics of a location can dictate which individuals are more likely to fall prey to violent crime. Urban areas, often characterized by higher crime rates, may reflect a cultural desensitization to violence, leading to a greater likelihood of victimization for those who do not conform to societal expectations. Conversely, rural areas might exhibit different cultural norms that prioritize community cohesion, creating a unique set of potential victims based on local attitudes and relationships. This geographic lens highlights how cultural context can shape the risk factors associated with victim selection.

Social dynamics also play a crucial role in the vulnerability of potential victims within a cultural framework. Factors such as social isolation, power differentials, and community support systems can either protect or expose individuals to the threat of violence. In cultures where collectivism is emphasized, for example, individuals may experience a heightened sense of security due to strong community ties. In contrast, cultures marked by individualism may leave individuals more vulnerable, as the lack of social support can increase isolation and decrease the likelihood of intervention in potentially dangerous situations. These social dynamics are essential for understanding how cultural contexts influence victim selection.

Historical case studies illuminate the complex interplay between culture and victim selection, offering insights into the patterns of violence across different eras and societies. An examination of notorious murder cases reveals that the cultural backdrop often informs the offender's choice of victim, exposing underlying societal tensions and biases. By analyzing these historical instances, true crime enthusiasts can gain a deeper appreciation for how cultural influences have shaped not only the behavior of offenders but also the narratives surrounding victims, ultimately enriching their understanding of the multifaceted nature of victimology.

# CHAPTER 6

# Historical Case Studies of Victim Choice

*Notorious Historical Figures and Their Victims*
Notorious historical figures have often left a profound impact on society, not only through their criminal acts but also through the complex dynamics of victim selection. Understanding these dynamics requires delving into the psychological profiles of their victims, as well as the social and geographic factors that influenced these choices. Figures such as Jack the Ripper and H.H. Holmes exemplify how specific characteristics of victims, often linked to social vulnerability, made

them more accessible targets. These historical cases offer insights into the dark interplay between the perpetrator's motivations and the victim's circumstances.

The psychological profiles of potential victims reveal much about the vulnerabilities that criminals exploit. Victims often share common traits, such as marginalized social status, lack of protective resources, or being in transient situations. The victims of Jack the Ripper, for instance, were largely women of lower socioeconomic status, highlighting how the intersection of gender and social class can create a fertile ground for predation. By analyzing such profiles, true crime enthusiasts can gain a deeper understanding of the motivations that underpin victim selection, emphasizing the need for awareness of these vulnerabilities in contemporary society.

Geographic considerations also play a crucial role in victim selection. Notorious criminals often target specific areas that align with their modus operandi and the demographic composition of potential victims. H.H. Holmes, who operated in Chicago during the World's Fair, strategically chose his victims from the influx of visitors, capitalizing on their unfamiliarity with the area and their transient status. The geographic context not only influences the availability of victims but also impacts the opportunity for crimes to occur, reflecting a critical aspect of victimology.

Social dynamics further complicate the landscape of victim vulnerability. Historical figures like Ted Bundy managed to manipulate social perceptions and trust, often targeting individuals who conformed to societal ideas of safety and normalcy. This manipulation indicates that victim choice is not solely a matter of opportunity but also involves an understanding of social hierarchies and the perceived safety of various demographic groups. The case studies of such criminals highlight the intricate relationship between societal norms and the ease with which certain individuals can become targets.

The role of technology in modern contexts adds another layer to the discussion of victim selection. While historical criminals relied on physical proximity and social manipulation, today's perpetrators may exploit digital platforms to identify and target victims. The evolution of technology has created new opportunities for offenders, making certain individuals more accessible and vulnerable than ever before. This shift prompts a reevaluation of historical patterns and their relevance to contemporary victimology, emphasizing the need for vigilance in an increasingly interconnected world.

*Patterns in Historical Victim Selection*

Patterns in historical victim selection reveal a complex interplay of psychological, social, and environmental factors that have influenced the choices made by murderers throughout time. By examining these patterns, true crime enthusiasts can gain insights into the motivations behind such choices and the characteristics that make certain individuals more susceptible to becoming victims. Understanding these dynamics is crucial for recognizing the broader implications of victimization in society.

Psychological profiles of potential victims often highlight traits that can make individuals more appealing targets for predators. Historical patterns show that perpetrators frequently select victims based on perceived vulnerabilities, such as mental health issues, socio-economic status, or isolation. This selection process is not random; rather, it reflects the murderer's own psychological makeup, including their need for control or domination. By studying these profiles, enthusiasts can grasp the chilling reality that many victims share common psychological traits that can be exploited by those with malicious intent.

Geographic considerations play a significant role in victim selection, as the environment shapes both the opportunities for crime and the demographics of potential victims. Historical analyses reveal that urban areas, with their anonymity and density, often present more opportunities for murderers than rural settings. Furthermore, specific neighborhoods may be characterized by higher crime rates, making residents more vulnerable. By understanding these geographic patterns, one can appreciate how location influences not only victim selection but also the overall dynamics of crime in different contexts.

Social dynamics significantly contribute to victim vulnerability, as societal structures can either protect or expose individuals to danger. Historical case studies demonstrate that marginalized groups, including women, minorities, and the economically disadvantaged, are often disproportionately targeted. The interplay of power, privilege, and societal norms shapes the landscape of victimization, making it essential to consider these factors when analyzing why certain individuals become victims while others do not. This understanding can enhance awareness and preventative measures within communities.

Finally, the role of opportunity in victim selection cannot be overstated. Historical patterns indicate that many murderers exploit situational factors, such as lack of supervision, accessible locations, or specific events that create a sense of normalcy, allowing them to act without immediate suspicion. Moreover, advancements in technology have transformed the landscape of victim accessibility, with digital footprints and social media presenting new avenues for offenders. By examining these historical case studies and the factors influencing victim selection, true crime enthusiasts can develop a deeper understanding of the complexities surrounding murder choices and the ever-evolving nature of victimization.

*Lessons Learned from Past Cases*

Lessons learned from past cases reveal critical insights into the factors influencing victim selection in murder scenarios. One of the most significant lessons is the interplay between psychological profiles and victim choice. Historical cases often illustrate that perpetrators tend to target individuals who exhibit specific traits or vulnerabilities. For instance, victims may be chosen based on perceived weaknesses, such as low self-esteem or social isolation. Understanding these psychological profiles helps to identify patterns and develop preventative strategies in contemporary victimology.

Geographic considerations also play a pivotal role in how murderers select their victims. Analyzing past cases reveals that location can significantly influence victim accessibility. Urban areas may present a higher likelihood of anonymity for offenders, making it easier for them to blend into the surroundings after committing a crime. Conversely, rural settings may offer fewer opportunities due to the close-knit nature of communities. By examining geographical patterns in historical cases, investigators can better understand crime hotspots and enhance community awareness and safety measures.

Social dynamics and victim vulnerability are intricately connected to the choice of murder victims. Historical case studies show that social relationships, such as familial ties or romantic connections, often lead to tragic outcomes. Victims may be selected based on their relationship with the perpetrator, where trust and familiarity can create an illusion of safety. This dynamics highlight the need for broader societal education regarding the complexities of interpersonal relationships and the potential dangers they can harbor, encouraging communities to foster awareness and vigilance.

The impact of technology on victim selection has evolved dramatically over the years, as evidenced by various historical cases. With the rise of social media and digital communication, offenders can now easily gather information about potential victims, identifying their routines and vulnerabilities. Cases from the past illustrate how technology has created new avenues for stalking and manipulation, emphasizing the importance of digital literacy in personal safety. Educating individuals about the risks associated with their online presence can serve as a crucial preventative measure against victimization.

Finally, the role of opportunity in victim selection cannot be overstated. Historical case studies consistently indicate that murderers often act on impulse when the opportunity arises, rather than through premeditated plans. This underscores the importance of situational awareness and environmental factors in victim selection. By learning from past cases, communities can implement strategies to reduce opportunities for crime, such as improved lighting, surveillance measures, and neighborhood watch programs. Understanding the lessons from these cases empowers individuals and communities to take proactive steps in minimizing the risk of victimization.

# CHAPTER 7

# The Role of Opportunity in Victim Selection

*Situational Crime Prevention*

Situational crime prevention focuses on reducing opportunities for crime through environmental and behavioral modifications. It operates under the principle that crime is not merely a result of individual predispositions or societal factors but is significantly influenced by the specific context in which it occurs. By understanding the factors that contribute to victim selection, true crime enthusiasts can gain insights into how potential victims are often targeted based on their situational vulnerabilities. This approach emphasizes the importance of recognizing patterns in crime, which can help in developing strategies to deter offending behavior.

One key aspect of situational crime prevention is the role of environmental design. Geographic considerations play a vital role in victim selection, as certain locations present more opportunities for potential offenders. Areas that are poorly lit, isolated, or lack natural surveillance are more likely to attract criminals seeking vulnerable targets. Crime prevention strategies often involve improving the physical environment, such as enhancing street lighting, increasing police presence, and implementing community watch programs, all of which can significantly reduce the likelihood of victimization.

Psychological profiles of potential victims are also crucial in understanding situational crime prevention. Offenders often select victims based on observable traits or behaviors that signal vulnerability. For instance, individuals who display signs of distraction or intoxication may be perceived as easier targets. By analyzing historical case studies, true crime enthusiasts can identify patterns in victim behavior and characteristics, enabling them to understand how certain psychological traits can increase the likelihood of becoming a target. This understanding can inform preventive measures that encourage individuals to adopt behaviors that reduce their vulnerability.

Social dynamics further complicate the victim selection process, as relationships and interactions within communities can either enhance or diminish the risk of victimization. Offenders may exploit social situations, such as parties or public gatherings, to identify potential victims. Factors such as group dynamics, peer influence, and socio-economic conditions can all play a significant role in determining who becomes a target. Situational crime prevention strategies can incorporate community engagement efforts to foster stronger social ties, thereby reducing the likelihood of individuals becoming isolated and vulnerable.

Finally, the impact of technology on victim accessibility cannot be overlooked in the context of situational crime prevention. The rise of digital platforms has created new avenues for offenders to identify and select victims, particularly through online interactions. Cyberstalking and online grooming are modern manifestations of how technology can facilitate victimization. Educating the public about safe online practices and promoting awareness of digital vulnerabilities are essential components of situational crime prevention. By addressing both physical and digital environments, strategies can be developed to protect potential victims from the evolving landscape of crime.

### The Importance of Timing

The concept of timing is critical in understanding the dynamics of murder choices and victim selection. In the realm of victimology, the timing of an attack often reflects a confluence of various factors, including the perpetrator's psychological state, societal conditions, and the victim's circumstances. The decision to act may hinge on a fleeting moment of opportunity, where the perpetrator perceives a vulnerability in the victim, or it may be the result of meticulous planning over an extended period. True crime enthusiasts can gain deeper insights into these dynamics by examining specific cases where timing played a pivotal role in the outcome of violent acts.

Psychological profiles of potential victims often reveal that certain individuals are more susceptible to being targeted based on their routines and behaviors. For instance, victims who maintain predictable schedules or engage in solitary activities may present themselves as more accessible during specific times of day. Perpetrators frequently exploit these patterns, choosing moments when victims are least likely to be surrounded by protective social structures. Analyzing cases where timing was a decisive factor illustrates how perpetrators capitalize on these vulnerabilities, reinforcing the need for heightened awareness of one's surroundings at various times.

Geographic considerations also significantly influence the timing of victim selection. Urban environments may provide different opportunities compared to rural areas, with the density of population and the anonymity of city life allowing for greater concealment of criminal acts. The timing of a crime can be strategically aligned with the geographical context; for example, the cover of darkness in poorly lit neighborhoods can embolden offenders. Historical case studies demonstrate how certain locales have become hotspots for specific types of crimes, often dictated by the timing of when individuals are most exposed due to societal rhythms.

Social dynamics play a crucial role in victim vulnerability, particularly concerning timing. Social gatherings, public events, and even routine activities can create windows of opportunity for offenders. Victims may be more susceptible during times of emotional distress, such as following a breakup or during significant life changes, which can be exploited by those with malicious intent. Furthermore, the concept of "social time," where individuals lower their guard in familiar settings, is relevant in understanding why certain times can be particularly dangerous for specific demographics, highlighting the intricate relationship between social interactions and victim selection.

The impact of technology on victim accessibility cannot be overlooked when discussing the importance of timing. With the rise of social media and location-based applications, individuals often inadvertently broadcast their whereabouts, making it easier for potential offenders to track their movements. Timing becomes even more critical in this context, as perpetrators can take advantage of real-time information to choose the most opportune moments to strike. The evolution of forensic evidence collection has also changed the landscape of victim selection, emphasizing the need for both potential victims and law enforcement to understand not just the "who" and "how," but also the "when" of murder choices.

*Accessibility and Its Impact on Victim Choice*

Accessibility plays a crucial role in determining victim choice within the context of murder. This concept encompasses not only physical proximity but also the social and psychological factors that influence a potential perpetrator's decision-making process. Understanding how accessibility affects victim selection can illuminate patterns that might otherwise remain obscured when examining cases in isolation. By analyzing the interplay between location, social dynamics, and victim vulnerability, we can gain insight into the broader mechanisms that drive individuals toward specific targets.

Geographic considerations significantly impact victim accessibility. Perpetrators often select victims based on their presence in certain areas, such as neighborhoods with higher crime rates or locations where individuals may be less likely to receive immediate assistance. Urban environments, with their dense populations and anonymity, can provide a facade of safety for a criminal, allowing them to blend in more easily after committing a crime. In contrast, rural settings may offer fewer opportunities but can also present a false sense of security for victims who believe they are safe from harm. This geographic interplay forms a critical foundation for understanding why certain individuals become targets.

Social dynamics further complicate the issue of victim accessibility. Factors such as socioeconomic status, gender, and community relationships can all influence how vulnerable individuals become to potential predators. For instance, those who are socially isolated or lack strong support networks may be more easily targeted. Additionally, the demographic characteristics of a community can shape patterns of victimization, as perpetrators may gravitate toward individuals who fit certain psychological profiles. Understanding these dynamics helps to illustrate the different layers of accessibility that can lead to tragic outcomes.

The evolution of technology has also transformed the landscape of victim accessibility. The rise of social media and online platforms has created new avenues for perpetrators to identify and groom potential victims. Digital footprints can reveal personal information, making individuals more accessible than ever before. Furthermore, advancements in surveillance technology can either hinder or facilitate a perpetrator's ability to commit a crime undetected. This duality highlights the necessity for individuals to remain aware of their digital presence and the implications it may have for their safety.

Historical case studies provide compelling evidence of how accessibility has affected victim choice in notorious murder cases. Analyzing these instances reveals recurring themes in victim selection, often pointing to a predator's calculated approach to identifying and exploiting vulnerabilities. By examining the circumstances surrounding these cases, true crime enthusiasts can uncover the intricate balance between opportunity, accessibility, and the chilling reality of murder. This exploration not only enhances our understanding of victimology but also serves as a reminder of the importance of awareness and prevention in today's society.

# CHAPTER 8

# Gender and Demographics in Target Selection

*Gender-Specific Victim Patterns*

In analyzing gender-specific victim patterns, it becomes evident that certain demographic factors play a crucial role in how perpetrators select their targets. Historically, studies have shown that men are more often the offenders in violent crimes, while women frequently become the primary victims. This gendered dynamic is not merely a statistical anomaly; it reflects deep-seated social structures and cultural perceptions about gender roles. For instance, many male offenders may view women as symbols of vulnerability or as easier targets, often leading to a disproportionate representation of female victims in violent crime statistics.

Psychological profiles of potential victims reveal that societal norms surrounding gender can significantly influence vulnerability. Women, often socialized to prioritize nurturing and caretaking roles, may inadvertently position themselves as targets by engaging in behaviors that are perceived as less assertive or defensive. Furthermore, the historical context of victimization, where women have been objectified and dehumanized, contributes to the persistence of these patterns. Understanding the psychological ramifications of such socialization can provide insights into why certain individuals become victims more frequently than others, particularly within specific gender contexts.

Geographic considerations further complicate the understanding of gender-specific victim patterns. Urban areas, for example, often present a higher incidence of violent crime, where demographic density can create both opportunity and anonymity for offenders. Women in these environments may be more susceptible to becoming victims due to factors such as their increased likelihood of using public transportation or being out late at night. Additionally, rural areas, while often perceived as safer, can also harbor their own unique risks, such as isolation that may amplify the vulnerability of women in those communities.

Social dynamics also play a pivotal role in shaping victim vulnerability along gender lines. The influence of peer groups, familial structures, and community expectations can dictate the behaviors and choices of individuals, often placing women in precarious situations. For example, social pressures may compel women to conform to certain expectations regarding dating or social interactions, which can expose them to predatory behaviors. Examining these dynamics reveals that the intersection of societal norms and individual choices significantly impacts the likelihood of becoming a victim.

Historical case studies of victim choice underscore the ongoing relevance of these gender-specific patterns. Notable cases reveal consistent themes of gender-based targeting, where male offenders often choose their victims based on perceived weaknesses linked to gender. The role of opportunity in victim selection is perhaps most pronounced in these instances, as the accessibility of potential victims is frequently determined by societal structures that privilege certain demographics over others. As technology continues to evolve, its impact on victim accessibility cannot be overlooked, with social media and online dating creating both new avenues for connection and new risks for those who may be unaware of the dangers inherent in these platforms.

### Age and Vulnerability Correlation

Age plays a critical role in the dynamics of victim selection, particularly in the context of murder. The correlation between age and vulnerability has been extensively documented in both criminological research and historical case studies. Younger individuals, especially children and teenagers, often exhibit a higher degree of vulnerability due to their limited life experience, physical defenselessness, and sometimes a lack of understanding of potential dangers. Conversely, the elderly may also present as vulnerable victims due to physical frailty, cognitive decline, or social isolation. This relationship between age and vulnerability underscores the importance of understanding demographic factors in the development of psychological profiles for potential victims.

When investigating the psychological profiles of murder victims, age is a significant variable that influences both the offender's choice and the overall circumstances surrounding the crime. Offenders may target younger individuals for various reasons, including a perceived ease of control or manipulation. Similarly, older victims might be chosen due to their established patterns of routine that can be exploited by offenders familiar with their daily lives. Understanding these psychological underpinnings helps to clarify why certain age groups are disproportionately represented among murder victims, illuminating the motivations that underpin these tragic choices.

Geographical considerations also play a vital role in the age-vulnerability correlation. Urban areas, with their diverse populations and anonymous environments, may provide offenders with more opportunities to target younger individuals who might be out late or engaged in risky behaviors. In contrast, rural areas may expose older individuals to greater vulnerability due to fewer community resources and social networks. The geographical context can shift the risk profile for different age groups, highlighting the interplay between location, age, and susceptibility to violent crime.

Social dynamics further complicate the relationship between age and vulnerability. Younger individuals often lack the social capital and networks that might provide protection from predatory behavior. Peer pressure, social media influence, and a quest for acceptance can lead to risky behaviors that increase exposure to danger. On the other hand, older adults may become victims due to exploitation by caregivers or financial fraud, highlighting how social relationships can create unique vulnerabilities at different life stages. By examining these social dynamics, we can better understand the situational factors that contribute to an individual's risk of becoming a victim.

Ultimately, the impact of technology cannot be overlooked in the age-vulnerability discourse. Digital advancements have created new avenues for offenders to target victims across age groups, from cyberstalking of young individuals to online scams aimed at the elderly. The accessibility of personal information through social media and other platforms has made it easier for perpetrators to identify and exploit vulnerable individuals. Understanding these technological influences is crucial for true crime enthusiasts and researchers alike, as they provide insights into modern victim selection strategies and the ongoing evolution of crime in society.

*Cultural Demographics and Target Preferences*

Cultural demographics play a pivotal role in understanding the preferences and choices made by murderers when selecting their victims. Analyzing the intersections of age, gender, ethnicity, and socioeconomic status reveals patterns that can inform both the motivations underlying these choices and the strategies employed by offenders. For instance, certain killers may gravitate towards victims who share similar demographic traits, believing this will afford them a sense of familiarity or ease when committing their crimes. Conversely, others might deliberately target individuals from different backgrounds as a means of exerting power or enacting their prejudices. By examining these demographic factors, true crime enthusiasts can deepen their understanding of the psychological underpinnings of victim selection.

Psychological profiles of potential victims often align closely with cultural demographics, as certain characteristics can render individuals more vulnerable to attack. Factors such as mental health status, lifestyle choices, and social circles contribute significantly to the likelihood of victimization. Offenders frequently exploit perceived weaknesses, targeting those who may be less likely to resist or report the crime. For example, individuals in marginalized communities often face heightened risks due to systemic issues such as poverty, lack of access to resources, and social isolation. By understanding these psychological profiles within the context of cultural demographics, enthusiasts can gain insights into the motivations of both victims and perpetrators.

Geographic considerations are equally essential in the analysis of victim selection. The environment in which an individual lives can greatly influence both the likelihood of victimization and the characteristics of potential targets. Urban areas, with their higher population densities and anonymity, may present more opportunities for offenders compared to rural settings, where community ties and visibility play a protective role. Furthermore, geographic factors such as crime rates and local policing practices can impact how and where murderers choose their victims. True crime enthusiasts can appreciate how these dynamics shape the landscape of potential victimization, revealing not just the choices of killers but also the vulnerabilities inherent in specific locales.

Social dynamics also significantly affect victim vulnerability, often intersecting with cultural demographics to create complex scenarios of risk. Factors such as peer influence, community cohesion, and societal norms can dictate who is perceived as a suitable target. For instance, individuals who are isolated or lack strong social networks may be more susceptible to becoming victims of violent crime. Additionally, cultural attitudes towards certain groups, informed by historical prejudices or societal stereotypes, can further exacerbate these vulnerabilities. True crime enthusiasts should consider how these social dynamics interplay with cultural demographics to illuminate the broader context of victimization.

Historical case studies provide vital insights into the patterns of victim choice, revealing trends that persist over time. By examining infamous cases and the demographics of the victims involved, enthusiasts can identify recurring themes related to cultural demographics and target preferences. The role of opportunity, often shaped by the societal landscape, emerges as a critical component in these narratives. As technology evolves, so too does the accessibility of potential victims, particularly in contexts such as online interactions and social media. Understanding how these factors converge allows true crime enthusiasts to appreciate the multifaceted nature of victim selection and the systemic issues that underlie these tragic events.

# CHAPTER 9

# The Impact of Technology on Victim Accessibility

*Cybercrime and Virtual Victimization*

Cybercrime has emerged as a significant concern in the realm of victimology, particularly as technology continues to evolve and integrate into every aspect of daily life. Virtual victimization encompasses a range of criminal activities conducted through digital platforms, including identity theft, cyberbullying, and online harassment. Unlike traditional forms of crime, virtual victimization often lacks the physical presence of a perpetrator, complicating the dynamics of victim selection and the psychological profiles of those targeted. Cybercriminals exploit perceived vulnerabilities, leveraging social media and other online interactions to identify potential victims who may be more likely to trust or engage with them.

The psychological profiles of potential victims in the context of cybercrime are multifaceted and often influenced by factors such as age, mental health, and social behavior. Younger individuals, particularly those who are active on social media, may display a higher propensity for sharing personal information, making them attractive targets for cybercriminals. Similarly, individuals who seek validation through online interactions might be more susceptible to manipulation. Understanding these psychological aspects offers insight into how certain individuals can be categorized as easier targets based on their online behavior and emotional states.

Geographic considerations also play a crucial role in the selection of victims for cybercrime. While virtual platforms transcend physical boundaries, certain regions may experience higher rates of cybercrime due to socioeconomic factors, levels of digital literacy, or law enforcement capabilities. Areas with limited access to technology or cybersecurity education may produce a demographic more vulnerable to online predation. Cybercriminals often exploit these geographic disparities by targeting individuals from regions known to have less protective measures or awareness about cyber threats.

Social dynamics significantly influence victim vulnerability in the digital landscape. The interconnectedness of online communities can create a false sense of security, leading individuals to engage in risky behaviors such as sharing sensitive information with strangers. Additionally, social hierarchies and peer pressure can contribute to victimization, as individuals may feel compelled to conform to group norms or face ostracization. The interplay between online social dynamics and individual behavior highlights the need for awareness and education regarding safe online practices, as ignorance can lead to increased susceptibility to cybercrime.

Historical case studies of virtual victimization reveal patterns that can inform future prevention strategies. Analyzing notable incidents of cybercrime provides insights into the methods employed by perpetrators and the characteristics of their victims. For instance, the rise of phishing schemes and ransomware attacks has shown that opportunity often drives victim selection, where criminals utilize timing and current events to craft convincing schemes. By understanding these historical contexts and the evolving tactics of cybercriminals, true crime enthusiasts can develop a deeper comprehension of the factors that contribute to victimization in the digital age, ultimately fostering a stronger sense of vigilance and preparedness against cyber threats.

*Social Media Influence on Targeting*

Social media has become a powerful tool in shaping behaviors and influencing decisions, including those related to targeting potential victims in murder cases. The constant connectivity provided by platforms like Facebook, Instagram, and Twitter allows perpetrators to gather extensive information about individuals, their routines, and their vulnerabilities. This accessibility to personal data creates a unique environment where potential victims can be assessed based on their online presence. The digital footprint left by social media users can reveal not only their interests and social circles but also their emotional states, making it easier for offenders to identify who might be more susceptible to manipulation or harm.

Psychological profiles of potential victims are intricately tied to social media interactions. Offenders often exploit the information shared online to evaluate a person's psychological resilience or social support systems. For example, individuals who frequently post about personal struggles, such as mental health issues or relationship problems, may inadvertently signal their vulnerability to potential predators. This has led to a growing concern about the implications of oversharing on social media, as it can inadvertently place individuals at greater risk of being targeted. The psychological insights gained from analyzing social media behavior can significantly inform a perpetrator's decision-making process regarding victim selection.

Geographic considerations in victim selection are also influenced by social media. Many platforms allow users to tag their locations, share check-ins, and post about events they are attending. This information can be valuable for offenders looking to identify potential targets in specific areas, especially in urban environments where anonymity is often more easily maintained. The ability to pinpoint a victim's whereabouts in real-time enhances the opportunities for crime, as perpetrators can plan their actions based on the victim's online activity. Consequently, social media not only facilitates the identification of victims but also aids in the strategic planning of the crime itself.

Social dynamics play a crucial role in understanding victim vulnerability, particularly in the context of social media. Online interactions can create a false sense of security, leading individuals to underestimate potential threats. The phenomenon of cyberbullying and online harassment illustrates how social media can embolden aggressors and diminish the perceived risks of targeting certain individuals. Victims may feel isolated or unsupported due to the nature of their online interactions, which can be manipulated by offenders to further isolate them. This manipulation of social dynamics highlights the need for awareness of how online behavior can affect personal safety.

Historical case studies illustrate the impact of social media on victim choice in murder cases. Analyzing cases where social media played a significant role can provide insights into how technology has evolved the landscape of victim targeting. For instance, high-profile cases involving social media stalking or the use of online platforms to lure victims demonstrate the shifting dynamics of crime. These studies underscore the importance of understanding the intersection between technology and human behavior, as offenders increasingly leverage social media tools to facilitate their crimes. As society continues to navigate the complexities of digital interactions, it is essential to remain vigilant about the potential risks posed by social media in the context of victimology.

*Surveillance and Its Role in Modern Crime*

Surveillance has become an integral component of modern policing and crime prevention, significantly influencing the dynamics of victim selection. The proliferation of technology, including CCTV cameras, drones, and mobile tracking, has transformed not just how crimes are investigated but also how they are perpetrated. Criminals often find themselves navigating a landscape heavily monitored by both public and private entities. This omnipresence of surveillance alters the calculus of victim selection, as potential offenders must now consider the likelihood of being caught in the act and the increased scrutiny on their movements.

In the context of victimology, understanding how surveillance impacts crime can provide insights into the psychological profiles of potential victims. Those who are aware of surveillance measures may adopt behaviors that reduce their vulnerability. Conversely, individuals who perceive themselves as being in safe environments may let their guard down, inadvertently becoming more attractive targets. For example, a person who regularly uses poorly lit alleyways may not consider their surroundings, while another who is aware of nearby surveillance cameras may take precautions, demonstrating the psychological interplay between awareness and victimization.

Geographic considerations are also essential when discussing surveillance's role in modern crime. Urban areas, with their dense populations and extensive CCTV networks, create a different landscape for criminals compared to rural settings. Offenders may gravitate towards locations where they believe surveillance is minimal or where they can blend in with the crowd. This geographic awareness can influence not only where crimes occur but also the types of victims selected, as individuals in less monitored areas may be perceived as easier targets. The spatial dynamics of surveillance thus play a crucial role in determining victim accessibility.

Social dynamics and vulnerabilities are further compounded by the presence of surveillance technology. Certain demographics may feel more threatened by surveillance, either due to past experiences or societal narratives that stigmatize them. This can lead to a chilling effect, where individuals alter their behavior out of fear of being watched or judged. In contrast, those who feel secure in their environments may not recognize the potential risks, making them susceptible targets. The interplay between social perceptions of surveillance and individual vulnerability highlights the complexities of victim selection in a monitored world.

Historical case studies provide valuable context for understanding the evolving relationship between surveillance and crime. Notable cases illustrate how the introduction of surveillance technology has influenced criminal behavior and victim choice over time. For instance, in the wake of enhanced surveillance in urban centers, criminals may have shifted their tactics, opting for targets in less monitored suburban or rural areas. Analyzing these shifts reveals not only the changing landscape of crime but also emphasizes the critical role surveillance plays in shaping the choices of both offenders and victims alike. As technology continues to advance, so too will the strategies employed by those who seek to exploit vulnerabilities in an increasingly monitored society.

# CHAPTER 10

# Forensic Evidence and Victim Selection Strategies

*Understanding Forensic Psychology*

Understanding forensic psychology is crucial in the realm of victimology, particularly for those intrigued by the complexities behind murder choices. Forensic psychology bridges the gap between psychology and the legal system, providing insights into the behaviors and motivations of both offenders and victims. This discipline explores the psychological factors that influence criminal behavior, including the selection and targeting of victims. By understanding these elements, true crime enthusiasts can better appreciate the intricacies of how and why certain individuals become victims in the context of violent crime.

One of the primary focuses of forensic psychology is the development of psychological profiles for potential victims. This involves analyzing various traits that may make an individual more susceptible to being targeted. Factors such as age, gender, socioeconomic status, and lifestyle choices can significantly influence a person's vulnerability. For instance, certain offenders may seek out victims who exhibit specific characteristics, such as those who appear to be less socially connected or who frequently engage in risky behaviors. By understanding these psychological profiles, enthusiasts can gain a deeper insight into the dynamics of victim selection and the inherent risks associated with certain lifestyles.

Geographic considerations also play a pivotal role in victim selection, informed by the principles of forensic psychology. The environment in which a potential victim resides can affect their likelihood of being targeted. Offenders often choose victims based on accessibility, familiarity with the area, and the perceived risks involved in committing the crime. For example, urban settings may present a higher number of potential victims due to population density, while rural areas might offer less anonymity but more opportunity for targeted individuals. Analyzing geographic patterns helps enthusiasts understand the spatial dynamics at play in victim choice and the psychological factors that influence these decisions.

Social dynamics significantly contribute to victim vulnerability, a topic that forensic psychology addresses extensively. The relationships individuals maintain can either protect them or expose them to risk. Those who are isolated or lack strong social support systems may be more attractive targets for offenders. Furthermore, the psychological effects of societal norms and peer influences can impact an individual's behavior and choices, making them more susceptible to victimization. Understanding these social dynamics allows true crime enthusiasts to consider how societal structures and personal relationships influence the likelihood of becoming a victim.

Historical case studies provide a rich context for understanding the role of opportunity in victim selection. By examining infamous cases, forensic psychology reveals patterns and trends in how offenders choose their victims. These studies often highlight the intersection of opportunity, psychological predispositions, and situational factors. The evolution of technology has also transformed victim accessibility, with advancements creating new avenues for offenders to exploit. By exploring these historical perspectives, enthusiasts can draw connections between past and present victimization trends, enhancing their understanding of the complex psychological landscape that underpins the phenomenon of murder choice.

*How Forensic Evidence Influences Victim Choice*
Forensic evidence plays a crucial role in understanding how potential victims are chosen in murder cases. This subchapter explores the intricate relationship between the characteristics of forensic evidence and the selection of victims by offenders. Forensic evidence encompasses various scientific methods that aid in criminal investigations, from

DNA analysis to fingerprinting and digital forensics. These tools not only help solve crimes but also inadvertently shape the strategies employed by criminals when selecting their targets. Analyzing the implications of forensic evidence can illuminate trends in victim choice and highlight the vulnerabilities that certain individuals may possess.

One significant aspect of forensic evidence influencing victim choice is the psychological profile of potential victims. Offenders often select victims who exhibit traits that make them more vulnerable or easier to access. For instance, individuals with predictable routines, low self-esteem, or a lack of social support can be prime targets. Forensic evidence can reveal patterns in these selections by examining past crimes, identifying the common characteristics of victims, and analyzing how offenders exploit these traits. Understanding the psychological profiles that attract criminals can aid in developing preventive strategies and enhance community awareness.

Geographic considerations also play a pivotal role in victim selection. Forensic evidence can provide insights into the spatial dynamics of crime, revealing how offenders may choose victims based on location. Certain areas may be more prone to specific types of crimes due to socio-economic factors, law enforcement presence, or urban design. Forensic investigations often highlight these geographical patterns, indicating that offenders may gravitate towards locations where they perceive less risk of apprehension or where potential victims are more accessible. This geographic analysis can assist law enforcement and communities in identifying high-risk areas and implementing preventive measures.

Social dynamics and victim vulnerability are further influenced by forensic evidence. The presence of forensic markers at crime scenes can reflect broader societal issues, including the intersectionality of gender, race, and class. Offenders may target individuals based on perceived societal hierarchies, with certain demographics deemed more vulnerable. Forensic studies can reveal trends in victimization, showing how societal structures impact victim selection. By examining historical case studies, it becomes evident that understanding these dynamics is crucial for both prevention and support systems for potential victims.

Lastly, the impact of technology on victim accessibility cannot be overlooked. Advances in forensic science have changed how crimes are committed and how victims are chosen. The proliferation of digital footprints, surveillance technology, and social media has created new avenues for offenders to identify and target victims. Forensic evidence in cybercrime cases illustrates how technology can facilitate victim selection, enabling perpetrators to exploit personal information and create opportunities for crime. As technology continues to evolve, so too will the strategies employed by offenders, making it imperative to remain vigilant in understanding how forensic evidence influences victim choice in this ever-changing landscape.

*Case Studies of Forensic Impact on Victim Selection*

Case studies of forensic impact on victim selection reveal the intricate interplay between criminal psychology, opportunity, and social dynamics. Forensic science often uncovers patterns and trends that inform our understanding of why certain victims are chosen over others. Analyzing historical cases, we can identify how forensic evidence not only shapes investigations but also highlights the characteristics that make some individuals more vulnerable to becoming targets. This exploration can illuminate the psychological profiles of potential victims, allowing for a deeper comprehension of the motivations behind victim selection.

In examining notable cases, we find that geographic considerations play a significant role in victim selection. Criminals often operate within familiar environments, where they can assess potential targets with ease. For instance, serial killers may choose victims from specific neighborhoods that reflect their own backgrounds or social circles, thus exploiting the trust and vulnerability embedded in those communities. Forensic data, including crime scene analysis and victimology, provide insights into how geography directly influences a perpetrator's choices. By mapping these patterns, investigators can better predict future victimization hotspots and potentially intervene before further crimes occur.

Social dynamics and victim vulnerability are also critical factors in understanding victim choice. Historical case studies illustrate that certain individuals—often those marginalized by society—are more likely to be selected. Forensic investigations frequently reveal that offenders may target victims who exhibit characteristics such as isolation, lack of support systems, or socioeconomic disadvantage. The psychological profiles formed from these analyses highlight that the social environment can create a landscape where certain individuals are deemed easier or more appealing targets for violence. This underscores the need for a societal shift towards recognizing and addressing the vulnerabilities of these populations.

The role of opportunity in victim selection cannot be overstated. Many forensic case studies indicate that the circumstances surrounding a crime often dictate the final selection of a victim. Factors such as time of day, location, and the presence of witnesses can significantly influence an offender's decision-making process. For instance, cases involving domestic violence often reveal that intimate partners are chosen due to both emotional and situational factors, with forensic evidence providing critical context for understanding these dynamics. This highlights the importance of situational awareness in victim prevention strategies.

Lastly, advancements in technology have transformed the landscape of victim accessibility in contemporary crime. The digital age has created new avenues for offenders to identify and target potential victims through social media and online interactions. Forensic evidence now encompasses digital footprints, which can reveal patterns of behavior and victim selection techniques. Historical case studies demonstrate how technology has both facilitated and complicated traditional victimology, offering new insights into how offenders exploit technological vulnerabilities. Understanding these trends is essential for true crime enthusiasts seeking to grasp the evolving nature of crime and the factors that influence victim choice.

# CHAPTER 11

# Conclusion and Future Directions

*Summary of Key Findings*

The study of victimology, particularly in the context of murder, reveals a complex web of factors influencing the selection of victims by perpetrators. One of the key findings is that psychological profiles play a significant role in determining who becomes a victim. Research indicates that certain personality traits, lifestyle choices, and social behaviors can make individuals more susceptible to being targeted. Understanding these psychological aspects helps illuminate why specific individuals are chosen over others, often revealing a predator's desire to exert control or fulfill specific fantasies.

Geographic considerations also emerge as a crucial element in the victim selection process. The analysis suggests that environmental factors, such as urban versus rural settings, significantly impact the likelihood of victimization. In densely populated areas, anonymity and accessibility often lead to higher rates of violent crime, whereas in rural environments, isolation may increase vulnerability. This geographic lens underscores the necessity of contextualizing victim selection within the spatial dynamics of crime, as location plays a pivotal role in both the perpetrator's choice and the victim's fate.

Social dynamics further complicate the narrative of victim vulnerability. The findings highlight how societal structures, such as socioeconomic status, gender, and community ties, contribute to an individual's risk of becoming a victim. Those in marginalized or economically disadvantaged positions often find themselves at greater risk due to a lack of resources and support systems. Furthermore, the interplay between social networks and victim selection reveals that certain groups may be targeted due to perceived weaknesses or lack of protection, emphasizing the need for a broader understanding of the societal influences at play.

Historical case studies provide crucial insights into the patterns of victim choice throughout different eras. Analyzing infamous murders from various time periods reveals that while some factors remain constant, others evolve based on cultural shifts and societal norms. For example, the motivations for victim selection in the past may differ significantly from contemporary trends, influenced by changes in technology, law enforcement practices, and public awareness. These historical perspectives enrich the dialogue on victimology, allowing true crime enthusiasts to appreciate the nuances of victim selection across time.

The impact of technology on victim accessibility has transformed the landscape of crime in unprecedented ways. From the rise of social media to the proliferation of data tracking, potential perpetrators now have access to a wealth of information that can inform their choices. The findings indicate that technology not only facilitates the identification of potential victims but also alters the dynamics of the predator-prey relationship. As such, understanding the intersection of technology and victim selection is essential for comprehending modern crime and developing effective preventative strategies. This multifaceted analysis serves to deepen the appreciation of the complexities surrounding victimology and the myriad factors that influence who becomes a target in the realm of murder.

### The Importance of Victim Awareness

The importance of victim awareness in the context of murder choices cannot be overstated, especially for true crime enthusiasts who seek a deeper understanding of the factors influencing victim selection. Victim awareness encompasses the recognition of risk factors that make individuals more susceptible to becoming targets. By examining these vulnerabilities, investigators and researchers can gain insights into the psychological and situational elements that lead to certain individuals being chosen over others. Understanding victim awareness not only aids in predicting potential outcomes but also fosters a more empathetic perspective towards those affected by violent crime.

Psychological profiles play a crucial role in understanding victim selection. Offenders often target individuals who exhibit specific traits or behaviors that align with their own psychological needs. For example, individuals who display vulnerability, such as low self-esteem or isolation, may be more appealing to perpetrators seeking control or dominance. True crime enthusiasts can benefit from analyzing these profiles, as they provide a framework for understanding the predator-prey dynamic that often plays out in violent crimes. Awareness of these psychological factors contributes to a broader understanding of the complexities surrounding victimization.

Geographic considerations also significantly influence victim selection. Certain locations may present more opportunities for offenders, including secluded areas or neighborhoods with lower levels of surveillance. Analyzing geographical patterns helps to pinpoint hotspots where crimes are more likely to occur, thus enhancing victim awareness. True crime enthusiasts can explore historical case studies that illustrate these geographic considerations, revealing how certain areas have become infamous for particular types of violent crime. This knowledge aids in understanding the interplay between environment and victim vulnerability.

Social dynamics further complicate the landscape of victim selection. Factors such as socioeconomic status, community ties, and social networks can increase or decrease vulnerability. Individuals who lack strong social support or live in transient environments may find themselves at greater risk. By examining these dynamics, true crime enthusiasts can better understand how social structures contribute to victimization. This awareness not only enriches the analysis of past cases but also informs contemporary discussions about crime prevention and victim support.

Finally, the impact of technology on victim accessibility is a modern consideration that true crime enthusiasts must grasp. The advent of social media and online platforms has changed how offenders identify and target potential victims. The digital footprint left by individuals can reveal personal information that increases their vulnerability. Awareness of these technological implications is essential for understanding how contemporary murder choices are made. By recognizing the evolving nature of victim selection in the digital age, enthusiasts can appreciate the complexities of victimology and its relevance in both historical and current contexts.

*Future Research in Victimology*

Future research in victimology holds significant promise for enhancing our understanding of the complex dynamics surrounding victim selection in murder cases. As the field evolves, researchers are increasingly focusing on the psychological profiles of potential victims. This exploration not only aims to identify common traits or behaviors that may render individuals vulnerable but also seeks to understand the cognitive processes that perpetrators might employ when choosing their targets. By delving into the motivations and characteristics that attract offenders to specific victims, future studies can provide deeper insights into preventive measures and protective strategies for at-risk populations.

Geographic considerations will also play a crucial role in future victimology research. Geographic profiling, which examines the spatial patterns of crime, can offer valuable data on how location influences victim selection. By analyzing crime trends in various neighborhoods and urban versus rural settings, researchers can identify hotspots where certain demographics may be more susceptible to becoming victims. This can inform law enforcement strategies and community outreach programs aimed at reducing victimization in these vulnerable areas. Furthermore, understanding the geographic distribution of crime can help in developing targeted prevention initiatives that address the unique needs of different communities.

Social dynamics and victim vulnerability will continue to be a focal point of inquiry. Future research should investigate how societal factors such as socioeconomic status, social networks, and community cohesion influence a person's risk of being targeted. The interplay between individual circumstances and broader societal issues can shed light on why certain groups are disproportionately affected by violence. By examining these social determinants, researchers can advocate for policies that strengthen community ties and support systems, thereby reducing the likelihood of victimization.

The advent of technology has transformed many aspects of daily life, including the ways in which individuals are targeted by offenders. Future studies will need to address the impact of digital communication, social media, and online interactions on victim accessibility. Understanding how technology can facilitate stalking, harassment, or predatory behaviors will be essential in crafting effective preventive measures. Additionally, researchers must explore the implications of emerging technologies, such as artificial intelligence and data analytics, in both victim selection processes and law enforcement strategies aimed at mitigating these risks.

Finally, the role of gender and demographics in target selection remains a critical area for future exploration. Research should focus on how gender, age, race, and other demographic factors influence victimization patterns, as well as how societal perceptions of these factors shape offenders' choices. By examining historical case studies of victim selection alongside contemporary data, researchers can draw connections between past and present trends in victimology. This comprehensive approach will not only enrich the academic discourse but will also provide practical insights for true crime enthusiasts and practitioners seeking to understand and combat the phenomenon of victimization in society.

* 9 7 9 8 3 3 0 5 2 4 3 2 7 *